Q. S. T. S. "LUSITANIA".

PROFILE.

SCALE ⅛' = 1 FOOT.

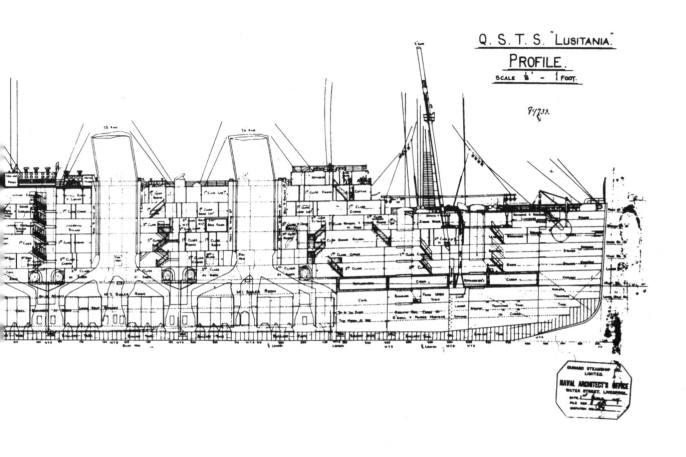

CUNARD STEAMSHIP CO.
LIMITED.
NAVAL ARCHITECT'S OFFICE
WATER STREET, LIVERPOOL.

40 50 60 70 80 90 100   200   300   400 FEET

HOLD PLAN.

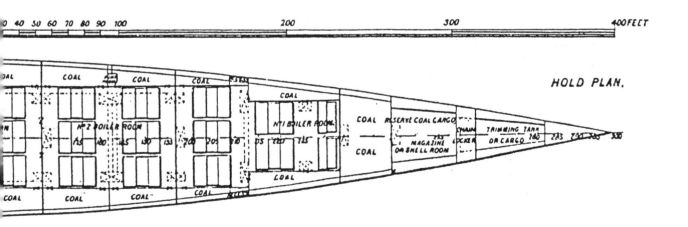

REMEMBER THE
LUSITANIA!

WALKER & COMPANY

NEW YORK

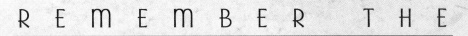

REMEMBER THE

LUSITANIA!

Diana Preston

For *Alice, Angus, Artemis, Clare, and Katy* —D. P.

First published in the United States of America in 2003 by Walker Publishing Company, Inc.

Every effort has been made to locate and contact all the holders of copyright to material reproduced in this book.

For information about permission to reproduce selections from this book, write to Permissions, Walker & Company, 435 Hudson Street, New York, New York 10014

Library of Congress Cataloging-in-Publication Data

Preston, Diana, 1952–
    Remember the Lusitania! / Diana Preston.
        p. cm.
    Summary: An account of the World War I German torpedo attack on and sinking of the passenger liner, the Lusitania, describing the experiences of some of those involved.
        ISBN 0-8027-8846-7—ISBN 0-8027-8847-5 (reinforced)
    1. Lusitania (Steamship)—Juvenile literature.   2. World War, 1914–1918—Naval operations—Submarine—Juvenile literature.   [1. Lusitania (Steamship)   2. World War, 1914–1918—Naval operations.]   I. Title.
    D592.L8 P75   2003
    940.4'514—dc21
                                                                2002027444

Book design by Maura Fadden Rosenthal/MSPACE

previous page:
Lusitania *on the Hudson River going past the New York skyline*

Souvenir log book

CONTENTS

Warning from German Embassy and Cunard ad in newspaper

DOOMED

It was raining on the morning of May 1, 1915—a thin, drizzling kind of rain that hung in the air like a mist. Droplets from his sodden hat dripped on the newspaper boy's face as he stood on the dock at Pier 54. He brushed them away before shouting "'Big Lusy' sailing today. American passengers travel at their own risk, warns German Embassy."

Cunard's spokesman, Charles Sumner, stared anxiously at the notice in the paper. It was surrounded by a thick black line and read:

> Travelers sailing in the war zone on ships of Great Britain
> or her allies do so at their own risk.

The notice was right next to the Cunard shipping line's own notice advertising the sailing of its ships from New York to Europe. It was signed by the Imperial German Embassy, Washington, D.C.

Sumner looked up at the huge ship anchored alongside the dock. The previous evening twenty-two trains had delivered the six thousand tons of coal needed to fill her vast bunkers. Grimy, sweat-soaked firemen had labored through the night feeding her furnaces to raise steam for the voyage ahead.

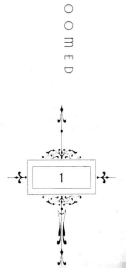

Now smoke was curling from three of her four great smokestacks. She looked awesome, magnificent, all eight hundred feet of her. She was the famous *Lusitania*, the "big Lusy," one of the fastest and certainly the most beautiful of all the ocean liners sailing the Atlantic. When she first sailed into New York on September 13, 1907, on her maiden voyage, she had caused a sensation. Now she was preparing for her 101st eastward crossing of the Atlantic Ocean to the British port of Liverpool. Gangways had already been lowered, waiting for the nearly 1,300 passengers to arrive. The big escalator was ready to start moving their trunks and cases aboard. But, Sumner wondered, what would happen now? Would people cancel their reservations?

In New York's hotels, anxious passengers discussed the newspaper notice. What did it mean? Was it really a warning that the *Lusitania*, a British ship, might be attacked by German ships or submarines? After all, Britain and Germany had been at war for nearly a year. Just a few weeks ago, in February, Germany had

announced that her submarines—or "U-boats," as the Germans called them—would sink without warning any British merchant ship they could. Some people now wondered anxiously whether they should transfer to another ship. The American liner *New York* was also sailing for Great Britain that day. Perhaps it would be wiser to travel on her. The United States was neutral in the war, so her ships should be safe from the submarines.

News reporters eager for a story hurried to the Cunard shipping line's offices near the docks to bombard staff with questions. Scribbling away in their notebooks, they demanded to know whether the *Lusitania* was in danger. A harassed Charles Sumner told them firmly, "The fact is that the *Lusitania* is too fast for any submarine. No German vessel of war can get near her." He also assured them that special agents and plainclothes policemen would be mingling with the crowds on the dock, looking for stowaways and other suspicious characters. Everything was being done to protect the ship.

Panorama of dock

As the hours passed, only a handful of nervous people decided to cancel their bookings. These included two friends who had nearly sailed on the *Titanic*, the liner that had hit an iceberg and sunk on her maiden voyage just three years earlier. It looked like the "Lusy" would be carrying over 1,250 passengers, including nearly 200 Americans, as well as her crew of 700. The voyage would be business as usual.

As the rain stopped and the sun came out, the docks sprang quickly to life. Bellboys who had been on shore leave came rushing back to the ship to get into their brass-buttoned uniforms. One of them, fifteen-year-old William Burrows, was stopped at the dock gates by a policeman who had just read the German warning. He told the startled boy, "You're not going to get back this time, sonny. They're going to get you this time." The puzzled teenager hurried on board, where a crewman told him about the warning. Another said that during the night the ship's cat, four-year-old black-furred Dowie, had run away. It seemed a bad omen. But what could they do except get on with their jobs? In a few hours the "big Lusy" would be leaving New York.

Before long the pier was overflowing with people. It was all bustle, excitement, and chaos as cars and horse-drawn carriages delivered passengers to the ship. Carts piled with steamer trunks and boxes clattered along, their harassed drivers yelling frantically at people to get out of the way. Photographers dodged about in the crowds, looking for departing celebrities to snap for the newspapers. It was always news when the "big Lusy" sailed, and the German warning made this occasion particularly newsworthy. Some photographers were even shouting, "Last pictures of the *Lusitania*!" as if they did not expect to see the ship again.

Loading

First-class passengers were gathering by the gangplank in the center of the ship. Their staterooms were here, "amidships." This was the best, most comfortable place to be in rough seas because it rocked and rolled the least. Other less well-off families struggled through the crowds and towers of baggage on the pier, trying to keep hold of their possessions and their children at the same time. They were looking for the gangplanks to the second- and third-class accommodations. Second-class passengers were supposed to board at the rear, or "stern," of the ship. Third-class passengers were to board at the front, known as the "bow." This was the least comfortable part of the ship, where people would feel every pitch and roll as the prow cut through the water.

Eleven-year-old Frank Hook, his twelve-year-old sister, Elsie, and their father, George, a widower in his mid-forties, were standing in the line of third-class passengers. George had sold his house in Toronto and was taking his children home to his native England. He had only paid half-fare for Elsie, although she was a year over age. Anxiously he told her to duck down and make herself look as small and young as possible when they got to the desk.

Formalities were taking longer than usual this morning because of the extra security. U.S. Secret Service men mingled with the noisy crowds. Their eyes flickered from face to face while passengers handed over their tickets and documents to Cunard officials who checked them with extra care. Passengers were then led to their bags, which they identified. The luggage was marked with chalk and then loaded onto the escalator. Private detectives were on the lookout for German secret agents trying to slip aboard with hidden weapons or explosives. Who knew what they might do once the ship was in the mid-Atlantic and far from help? They might even try to blow her up. But it was hard to keep track of everybody and everything in the confusion!

Twelve-year-old Avis Dolphin came hesitantly up the second-class gangway. Her father had died of tuberculosis, and her mother was sending her to school in England. She didn't want to go. At her side was Hilda Ellis, a young nurse from the nursing home Avis's mother ran in St. Thomas, Ontario, who would be looking after her for the next six days. But Avis was already feeling lonely and homesick. The voyage ahead held little magic. She knew Hilda wasn't really interested in her and was looking forward to having fun with any good-looking young men she could find.

Second-class stateroom

But as Avis stepped on board the *Lusitania,* she forgot her worries. Walking along elegant corridors in search of their stateroom, she and Hilda passed luxurious salons furnished with gold-colored wooden tables and deep sofas. Chandeliers with glass drops sparkling like diamonds hung from high stained-glass ceilings. Avis decided she was in "a floating palace."

The stateroom Avis was to share with Hilda and two other women was light and quite roomy, with berths surrounded by soft, thick curtains that could be closed to keep out the noise and "nosy" eyes. Their stewardess showed them where to stow their clothes and belongings so that they were out of the way and offered to bring them early-morning tea the next day, even breakfast in bed if they wanted.

Five decks down, right by the waterline, the Hooks were happily settling in. No one had asked awkward questions about Elsie's age, and their cabin was larger and more comfortable than they had expected. Third class on the *Lusitania* had the reputation of being better than on any other ship, and it seemed to be true. There were even automatically flushing toilets in the bathrooms down the corridor—something very rare in 1915.

First-class stateroom

First-class lounge

The *Lusitania* was most famous, though, for her fabulous first-class accommodations. The magnificent salons, staterooms, and suites were modeled on the great palaces of Europe. They didn't look as if they belonged on a ship at all, with their marble fireplaces, silken draperies, and thick, velvety carpets. This was where the famous, glamorous, and wealthy— the British lords and ladies, the American millionaires, the actors, actresses, and writers—would pass the voyage.

Handsome Alfred Vanderbilt, one of the richest men in America, was making himself comfortable in a lavish suite on the Boat Deck.

Alfred Vanderbilt

His valet, Ronald Denyer, was unpacking, so when a reporter, who had been authorized to come on board to interview celebrities, knocked on the door, the millionaire opened it himself. The pink carnation he always liked to wear was stuck neatly in the buttonhole of his charcoal-gray pin-striped suit. He was holding a telegram in his hand. The message read, "The *Lusitania* is doomed. Do not sail on her." It was signed "Morte"—"Death." The reporter asked Vanderbilt how he felt. The millionaire just shrugged, saying with a smile that it was probably "just someone trying to have a little fun at my expense." He had no intention of changing his plans.

American surgeon-major Warren Pearl, his wife, Amy, and their four young children had also booked one of the first-class suites. They had brought two nurses with them, Alice Lines and Greta Lorenson. Eighteen-year-old Alice's job was to look after tiny baby Audrey, just three months old, and five-year-old Stuart, while Greta cared for three-year-old Amy and two-year-old Susan. The Pearls knew that by traveling first class, their children could play in an exclusive nursery under the watchful eye of a spe-

Bridge of ship

cially trained stewardess. They could eat their meals in a fairy-tale dining room gilded and decorated to look like the palace of the French king Louis XVI.

Just after 11:30 A.M. bellboys began loudly banging gongs to warn anyone not sailing to go ashore. People who had come to say good-bye to friends and family gave them one last kiss and hurried down the long passages to get off the ship in time. Officers reported to the ship's bridge. A loud whistle announced that three tugboats were waiting to nudge the huge *Lusitania* out into the Hudson River. Passengers came pouring onto the open decks to wave good-bye, Avis Dolphin, Frank Hook, and the Pearl family among them.

As the *Lusitania*'s captain, Will Turner, stood on the ship's bridge with his officers by his side, dockworkers untied the thick ropes securing the *Lusitania* to the dock, and the tugs helped her back slowly out. Three ear-splitting blasts of her horn signaled farewell. Down on the dock people were waving hats, handkerchiefs, and flags, shouting and flinging fistfuls of confetti in the air. The ship's band played a lively tune at one end of the deck, while at the other end a men's choir from Wales who had been touring America sang "The Star-Spangled Banner."

Streamers of brightly colored flags fluttered from the *Lusitania*'s masts as she moved out into midstream and caught the breeze. Ahead of her as she sailed down the Hudson was the liner *New York,* but, the passengers joked, the "Lusy" was faster and would beat her to England.

Captain William Turner

These women are believed to be volunteer nurses sailing on the Lusitania *to help in the war in Europe*

Still, some people could not hide their nervousness as the New York skyline faded into the haze. One crewman was so jumpy that he ran up to a young bride, Lucy Taylor, who was proudly wearing a new hat lavishly trimmed with shining blue-and-green peacock feathers. He snatched it from her head and hurled it into the Hudson. When she angrily asked him why he had done that, he replied that peacock feathers on board ship always brought bad luck.

The *Lusitania* had one last job to do before she headed out into the Atlantic Ocean. Three British warships were patroling just outside American waters. Some British sailors rowed out from them, battling through the swells, with sacks of mail for England. They slung them aboard the liner, shouting their good wishes for her safe and speedy journey.

Last image of the Lusitania

Meanwhile, a man on the deck of one of the warships took a photograph of the *Lusitania*. Unknown to any of the two thousand people on board the beautiful liner, it would be one of the last pictures anyone would ever take of her. She would never see New York again.

CHAPTER TWO

SEASICKNESS AND STOWAWAYS

As the sun rose the next morning, the *Lusitania* sailed eastward into the dawn. High up on the ship's bridge, the helmsman squinted into the light as he gripped the wheel, holding her on course. While passengers slept on, a group of young bellboys ran laughing back to their quarters. They had spent a lively night gleefully electrocuting rats in the hold. As one of them, fifteen-year-old Ben Holton, boasted to a sailor, "We got some electric wires, we took off the insulation, and we laid there watching while the rats ran across them."

Now, the boys hurriedly put on their jackets and caps. Soon they would be racing around the ship carrying messages and running errands for passengers. They worked hard—sometimes sixteen hours at a stretch—but the tips were good. A successful bellboy could set himself up in a small business after a few transatlantic crossings—if he didn't spend the money first.

Stewards began carrying the first trays of early-morning tea to staterooms and drawing back the curtains. Sunlight flooded in through the portholes. It was a perfect day, bright and calm, with the barest whisper of wind. The blue-green Atlantic sparkled.

*Second-class
dining room*

Before long, hungry passengers were streaming toward the dining rooms, joking about how sea air improved their appetites.

But not Avis Dolphin. She had not felt too bad when she first got up. Now she barely noticed the elegant decor of the second-class dining room, or the lavish menu promising anything from haddock to corned-beef hash and hominy cakes topped with thick golden syrup. People ate bigger breakfasts in those days, and some were eagerly ordering kidneys, lamb chops, and fried potatoes. But just the smell of the food made Avis feel queasy. She was seasick.

Avis Dolphin   *Ian Holbourn*

Nurse Hilda Ellis suggested fresh air would make her feel better, so Avis went out on deck. The salty breeze on her face was cool, but the seesaw sensation was unsettling. Quickly she plopped herself down in a deck chair and tried not to look at the waves. Every time she did, she felt her stomach rise and fall in time with them. Maybe it would help if she closed her eyes.

Just then she had the feeling of being watched. She looked up to see a man in a tweed coat. He had penetrating eyes and a nice smile. He asked whether she was ill. Shyly she admitted she was feeling "rather miserable." To her surprise he invited her to explore the ship with him, telling her the best way to recover from seasickness was to take your mind off it.

The man told her all about himself as they walked along the Boat Deck, past the thirty-foot-long white-painted wooden lifeboats. His name was Professor Ian Holbourn. His wife and three little boys were waiting back home for him on the Scottish isle of Foula, and he missed them terribly. He had been on a lecture tour of the United States and had not seen them for months.

The professor was a keen sailor who knew all about ships. He showed Avis how the *Lusitania*'s four great smokestacks, rising seventy-five feet above the Boat Deck, were secured by steel wires

Image showing cables supporting smokestacks

to stop them from toppling over in high winds. He also told her how the ship was constructed from thousands of large, overlapping steel plates held together by 4 million rivets, weighing a total of 500 tons. The ship needed 65,000 gallons of water every minute to cool the engines, while 250 miles of cables linked her electrical systems, powering everything from boot-cleaning machines to ice-cream makers. Avis was amazed—everything about this ship seemed incredibly big!

The professor and Avis crossed the little bridge linking the second-class deck to the splendors of the first-class areas. No one stopped them as they walked down thick-carpeted corridors to the gilded metal cages of the passenger elevators near the Purser's Office. (A purser is the officer responsible for the passengers' accommodations and comfort—like a hotel manager, only at sea.)

A pile of leaflets on the Purser's Office counter caught Avis's eye. The leaflets' title was *The Origins and Issues of the Present War.* The professor picked one up and glanced through it. He explained that it was a British government note about the causes of the war. It was designed to convince foreign passengers of the justice of Britain's fight. He told Avis how sad he had felt when, nine months earlier, news of the war first reached him. Everyone had predicted it would be over by Christmas 1914, yet it was still going on. More than 3 million soldiers had already died, and no one could tell how long it would last.

But this morning passengers were more concerned about how to find their way around the vast ship than about the war. The busy Purser's Office staff were patiently explaining the layout of the six public decks to confused people. A few were unhappy about their accommodations. A tall lady from Connecticut with a pointed nose and a straw hat was complaining that her first-class stateroom was next door to "a very noisy family." She wanted another.

Moving on, Avis and the professor paused by the entrance to the great domed, two-tiered first-class dining room, where late breakfasters were still eating. Alfred Vanderbilt was sitting at the splendid captain's table, his famous pink carnation in his buttonhole even at breakfast time. He was talking to Charles Frohman, New York's most famous theater manager and the man who had first staged *Peter Pan* in the city. But Avis was much more fascinated by two beautiful women who came over to talk to Vanderbilt and Frohman. The professor told her they were both actresses. He had seen one of them in a show called *When Knights Were Bold.* Her name was Rita Jolivet. Avis reluctantly followed the professor away and down another long corridor. Through half-opened doors she glimpsed the luxurious first-class suites.

In one of these suites, nurse Alice Lines was dressing baby Audrey Pearl. She was planning to leave Stuart in the first-class nursery while she wheeled Audrey around the deck. There would be plenty of children for Stuart to play with. One of the stewardesses had told her that there were more than one hundred aboard—a record for the *Lusitania*. There was already talk of holding a beautiful baby competition.

Away in the bow and far from the gilt and glitter surrounding Alice and the Pearls, Frank Hook was also happy. He and his family were breakfasting, and the dining room was certainly living up to Cunard's boast that it was the best third-class restaurant on the Atlantic. The food was delicious, and there was a lot of it— oatmeal porridge with milk or syrup, followed by all kinds of tasty dishes, from boiled eggs to fried fish. The tables were laden with

plates of soft, crumbly white bread and dishes of jam and marmalade.

All around Frank, passengers were murmuring appreciatively, their mouths full. For many it was the best food they had tasted for a long time, and they were making the most of it, determined to get good value for their ticket money and cramming in as much as they possibly could. Some were already wondering expectantly what there would be for lunch. How much

Third-class dining room

would they need to exercise to make room for some more large helpings?

The Hooks' fellow passengers seemed pleasant enough. Frank and Elsie's father, George, had already made friends with a young New York engineer named Jack Welsh and a pretty young hatmaker named Gerda Nielson. Jack had met Gerda for the first time on deck as the *Lusitania* was sailing out of New York. They had joked and chatted for a long time, and the two of them were now planning to spend the morning together. There was also a harassed, tired mother, Annie Williams, sailing alone with her six children, three boys and three girls ranging in age from nine-year-old Edith to four-month-old baby David. Her husband had deserted her soon after the family had emigrated to America. She had heard he had gone back to England. Now she too was returning in the hope of tracking him down. She had had to sell all the family's furniture and other possessions to raise the fare, but even that had not been enough. Kindly neighbors in Plainfield, New Jersey, had taken up a collection to make up the rest. Seated nearby was an older woman, Elizabeth Duckworth, whose husband had recently died. She had decided to leave her work as a weaver in Taftville, Connecticut, and return to England, the land of her birth.

After breakfast Frank and Elsie went out onto the open deck to play. A seaman turned a rope for Elsie so she could skip. Later she and Frank hung over the rail, trying to spot the shiny bodies of porpoises leaping through the gentle Atlantic swell and watch-

*Children playing
jump rope on deck*

ing the ship's prow cut through the waves as she carried them far
out into the ocean.

But before long there were other things to think about. A
sensational rumor began to ripple through the ship, which Frank,
Elsie, and Avis overheard adults discussing excitedly. Three stowaways had been discovered hiding in a steward's pantry. The men,
who spoke only German, had been locked away in cells below the
waterline, where they could do no harm. When the *Lusitania*
docked in Liverpool they would be handed over to the police.

But were they really simple stowaways? They could be German
spies or saboteurs who had smuggled themselves on board to attack
the ship when she was far from land and helpless. Many thought

*Passengers playing
shuffleboard on deck*

back to the German warning in the newspapers and wondered uncomfortably whether there was any connection. Could the shadow of war really be falling over this lovely ship, alone out here in the wide blue sea?

"GOOD HUNTING!"

The German submarine *U-20* slipped out to sea from her base at Emden on the north coast of Germany on Friday, April 30, just one day before the *Lusitania* left New York. Her official orders were to sail to the waters outside Liverpool to attack British troopships carrying soldiers to the war in mainland Europe. However, as the *U-20*'s captain, thirty-year-old Walther Schwieger, well knew, there might be even bigger prey.

He was aware, from information about targets distributed in code by his commanders, that the *Lusitania* was about to set out across the Atlantic to her home port of Liverpool. Just six weeks earlier, in March, the commander of another submarine, the *U-27*, had missed the liner by just one day. Captain Wegener had been lying in wait for the *Lusitania* outside Liverpool, but his fuel had begun

U-20 *Captain Walther Schwieger*

Walther Schwieger
giving orders

to run low, forcing him to sail back to Germany before he got the chance to attack her. The *Lusitania*—the most famous ship in Britain's passenger fleet—would be a great prize for a U-boat captain. But who could tell what Schwieger's chances might be? The ocean was a vast place, and he might never encounter her.

Whatever happened in the days ahead, Schwieger would put the safety of his thirty-four crewmen first. Although he was one of the most successful of the U-boat commanders, he seldom took risks, and his men loved him for it. He understood just how dangerous life in a submarine could be. It was only ten years since Germany had decided to build a fleet of these "tin fish," as some German sailors nicknamed them. The *U-20* was one of the newest of Germany's U-boats— she could travel up to 5,000 miles and was well armed with seven torpedoes and a deck gun—but she was still fragile and small, just 200 feet long and 60 feet wide.

The voyage to Liverpool would be hazardous. British warships would be hunting German submarines. If they spotted the *U-20* close to the surface, they would try to run her down. A ship's prow could cut through a submarine like a knife through butter. It would be no safer for the *U-20* beneath the waves. Schwieger knew that when he reached British waters, he would have to dodge nets hung across harbors and other narrow stretches of water to trap submarines. His colleagues had told him that they were often "hung with mines like tomatoes on a vine."

Now, as the *U-20* slid through the cold waters of the North Sea at the start of her mission, a dog's excited barking mingled with the thudding of the diesel engines. Walther Schwieger had adopted a female dachshund his men had rescued after sinking the Portuguese ship she had been on.

Life on a submarine was uncomfortable as well as dangerous. The U-boatmen worked in cramped, stressful conditions. Every bit of space had to be used to store the equipment and food they would need on the voyage. There was butter under the bunks and sausages next to the grenades. Some men even had to share their bunks with the spare torpedoes.

Lack of fresh food and exercise wore them down. So did the lack of fresh air. When they were not on duty, U-boatmen were expected to lie down and sleep because they used up less air asleep than awake. When the U-boat was running underwater, the air soon became foul enough "to give you a headache you would never get over." It was also cold and clammy. This was because the temperature inside was higher than the temperature of the seawater outside, causing the moisture in the air to condense on the walls and trickle down. One U-boatman decided "it

Longitudinal and cross sections of U-20

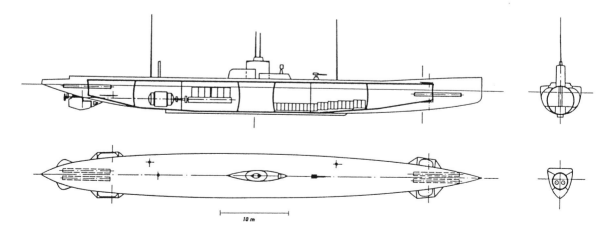

10 m

was really like living in a damp cellar." Men woke up choking and spluttering.

Another problem was that there was not enough water to wash in or to brush teeth properly, so that the crew soon stank of bad breath, sweat, and oil fumes. They had to wear the same leather clothes, day in, day out, sometimes for weeks on end. And they hardly ever shaved, becoming, as one said, as bearded and shaggy-haired as "the real pirates of old days."

The men also had to cope with unpredictable, temperamental toilets, which operated on a complicated system of valves and levers. If the user made a mistake, the toilet's contents blew back in his face. Submarine men called it "getting your own back." Also, it was not safe to flush the toilets when submerged in enemy waters during daylight, because the trail of frothing bubbles rising to the surface could give away the U-boat's position to waiting enemy ships.

But moments of pure magic made up for the hardships. At the order to dive—"Alarm! *Tauchen!*"—men leaped down the open hatchway, swinging the heavy conning-tower hatch shut behind them. A bell signaled shrilly that the hatch was sealed. Crewmen opened valves to let seawater pour into the submarine's diving tanks, and the U-boat tipped gently forward to begin her descent.

As she submerged, her crew would press their faces against the small side portholes to watch what one U-boatman described as the "foaming masses of water" that crashed over the bow. Next came "a confusion of bright foam and clear water outside the glass." As the submarine came to rest on the ocean floor amid a cloud of silver bubbles, schools of fish gathered to stare "with goggling eyes close to the windows in the turret." The inside of the U-boat seemed filled with a ghostly green light.

When it was time to rise again, the captain gave the order,

U-20 on the surface

"Surface stations." The chief engineer ordered his men to blow the seawater out of the diving tanks with compressed air. The submarine rose amid an "infernal din of hissing, roaring water." The men had to swallow to relieve the pressure in their ears. First the bow, then the whole deck, came up out of the sea. When the sailors finally opened the hatch, the fresh, tangy air streamed in. Fragments of jellyfish and strips of golden seaweed dangled from the steel ropes on deck.

Surfacing was a relief for the men, but it was also essential for operating the submarine. When submarines were underwater, they were powered by electricity produced by batteries. These batteries needed recharging often, but this could only be done when the U-boat was on the surface and using her main diesel engines.

Now, as the *U-20* sailed out of German waters, she met a German fishing boat whose sailors sold the U-boatmen fresh herrings. The fishermen bade them farewell with cheerful cries of "Good hunting!" Walther Schwieger replied, "Gott strafe England!"—"May God punish England"—and ordered the *U-20* to set course toward the northeast coast of Scotland. He ordered his radio operator to test his radio by sending a short message to a nearby German station. If conditions were good, he knew he would be able to stay in contact for up to five hundred miles. But once he was beyond that range, no orders could reach him. Neither could he seek advice from his commanding officer. The fate of the *U-20* and her crew would be entirely in his hands.

Danger came quickly. On only her second day at sea, the *U-20* had to dive to avoid a patrol of six British destroyers sailing straight toward her. Men flung themselves down the metal ladders and slammed the hatch shut, but it still took an agonizing seventy-five seconds to submerge. The *U-20* was lucky to escape.

Her relieved crew now sailed up around the coast of northern Scotland, threading through the islands and dodging further British patrols, before heading down the west coast of Ireland.

On May 5 Schwieger brought his small craft around the southern tip of Ireland and into the busy shipping lanes of the Irish Channel, to find thick fog. Schwieger knew that if he remained on the surface, he risked being smashed to pieces by a ship looming up unseen out of the mist. Cursing his bad luck, he gave the order to submerge. He could do nothing for a while but sit tight and wait.

But then his luck began to change. Resurfacing a while later, he found that the weather had cleared. He also found that a small British schooner, the *Earl of Lathom*, carrying bacon, eggs, and potatoes to Liverpool, was approaching. Shouting through a megaphone, he ordered her nervous crew to abandon ship. As soon as they had tumbled into their lifeboats and were frantically rowing away, he sank her with twelve shells from his deck gun. The next day, Thursday, May 6, he had even more success. Spotting the British steamer *Candidate*, he first shelled and then sank her with a torpedo, and then, just a few hours later, he torpedoed her sister ship, the *Centurion*. It looked as if the fishermen's wish of "good hunting" had been granted. But what should the captain do next?

Schwieger ordered the *U-20* to dive and head out to sea while he

Cover of Walther Schwieger's U-20 *war diary*

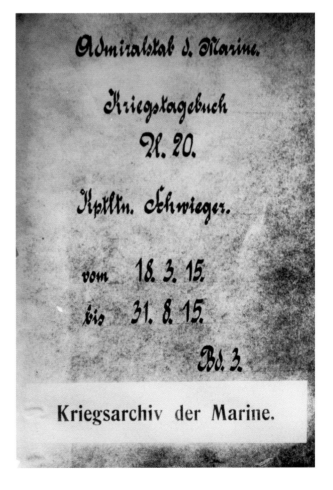

thought about it. Should he sail on to Liverpool, as he had been ordered? No. Schwieger now wrote in his log that this would use up too much fuel. Instead he would wait in the Irish Channel and attack ships there before returning to Germany. For those on the *Lusitania*, this would prove a fateful decision.

WATCHING AND WAITING

Aboard the *Lusitania*, the time was continuing to pass peacefully and uneventfully. The weather was still beautiful, with sunlit, cloudless skies. After the initial excitement most people had forgotten all about the German stowaways, who were being interrogated in their cell by ship's detective William Pierpoint. Out on deck, passengers played games, like egg-and-spoon races, laughing and urging each other on. Frank Hook was delighted to win a golden badge in the shape of the ship in one race. Others sat comfortably in deck chairs, wrapped in rugs, watching the changing colors of the sea.

Wealthy passengers were throwing parties at which glistening caviar was served out of swans sculpted from blocks of ice. Guests included rich Chicago manufacturer Charles Plamondon and his wife, Mary. Plamondon was afraid that Prohibition was coming to the United States, and he was traveling to Europe to try and sell his brewing equipment there. It would be his and Mary's wedding anniversary during the voyage, and they were planning to order champagne. At night, when dinner was over, the stewards pushed

Woman strolling with infant on deck

the tables aside, the band began to play, and people danced the latest dances, like the Turkey Trot and the Bunny Hug.

Avis Dolphin was enjoying her rambles around the ship with the professor more and more. She no longer felt shy and badgered him for stories of the Scottish isle of Foula, with its purple heathers and emerald green seas. He described how tiny it was—just five times the size of Central Park in New York—and made her laugh with his tales of the giants and bogeymen that he claimed lived on it.

Frank and Elsie Hook were now feeling thoroughly at home on the big ship and could find their way around without getting

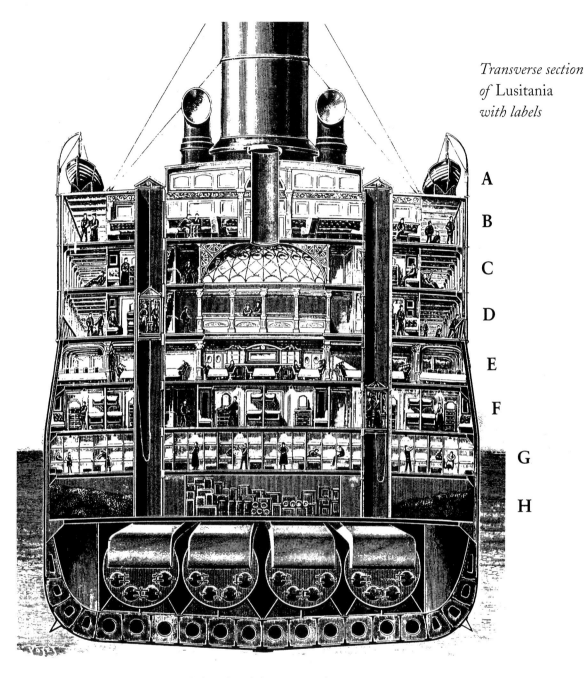

A
B
C
D
E
F
G
H

Life on board the *Lusitania* shown in section.
A: Boat Deck; B: Promenade Deck; C: Shelter Deck; D: Upper Deck;
E: Main Deck; F: Lower Deck; G: Orlop Deck; H: Lower Orlop.

lost. No one seemed to mind if they wandered into the first- and second-class areas. It was fun watching the seamen at work, painting the lifeboats with the gray paint they nicknamed "crab fat." It seemed a shame that in just a few days the voyage would be at an end, and there would be things like school to think about. Alice Lines was also enjoying the experience. The Pearls were a pleasant, friendly couple, and she was very fond of the children. Every evening, after she had put Audrey and Stuart to bed, the Pearls would invite her to have dinner with them in their private dining parlor.

Yet on the fourth day at sea, as the ship began to approach the British Isles, the mood changed. Avis and Frank noticed a growing unease and uncertainty creeping over the adults. At mealtimes they talked of little except what would happen when the *Lusitania* entered the Irish Channel. Would there be a German submarine attack? Would the British Navy send ships to escort her safely to Liverpool? Would the ship be diverted to the Irish port of Queenstown instead of sailing on to Liverpool?

Some people seemed excited by the thought of danger—one young woman hoped they would get "some kind of a thrill" as they entered the war zone—but many wondered anxiously how they would save their loved ones if anything should happen. Professor Holbourn was clearly concerned, promising Avis that in an emergency he would find her.

The professor was worried that the crew and passengers would be unprepared if the ship ran into danger. An experienced sailor himself, he told Avis that the passengers should at least know how to put their life jackets on. This seemed perfectly sensible to her, but he told her that when he had suggested this to

This life jacket from the Lusitania *washed up on the shore of the Delaware River, near Philadelphia, five years after the sinking.*

other male passengers, they had asked him not to keep on talking about the possibility of trouble "because it was upsetting the women passengers." The exasperated professor nicknamed them "the ostrich club," because, he said, they were exactly like ostriches who, when threatened, stupidly stuck their heads in the sand instead of doing something to save themselves.

Holbourn was also impatient with Captain Turner "because he refused to hold a lifeboat drill" for the passengers. A drill was a practice exercise teaching people exactly what to do and where to go in an emergency. During a drill passengers would be ordered

Lifeboats

to go to their cabins, put on their life jackets, and report to the lifeboats. He told Avis that the captain was afraid that a drill might cause panic or worry. There were drills for the crew, but these did not impress the professor or other watching passengers, although Frank and Elsie Hook enjoyed watching. At the sound of a few notes played by the ship's bugler, a group of crewmen ran up, climbed into a lifeboat, and sat in it for a few moments. Then they climbed out again. It seemed pointless.

On the other hand, at least there were plenty of lifeboats—twenty-two wooden ones and twenty-six boats with wooden bottoms but collapsible sides, which took up less space. The professor

Lusitania *at a high speed*

took Avis to inspect them. He showed her how the canvas sides of the collapsibles could be pulled up and braced. Unlike on the *Titanic*, there would be room in the lifeboats for everyone—passengers and crew—if the worst happened. There were also large quantities of big, bulky, fiber-filled life jackets that made their wearers look like padded football players. These were stowed in every cabin—Avis's was on top of the closet. If she climbed on her bunk, she could reach it quite easily. Notices stuck on the cabin walls instructed passengers how to put them on, but no one seemed to bother to read them.

Frank Hook's father was spending a good deal of time reassuring Elizabeth Duckworth and Annie Williams that they would be safe, although Frank and Elsie found it hard to believe that any harm could come to this enormous ship. Jack Welsh promised Gerda Nielson, with whom he was now deeply in love, that he

Stokers feeding coal into the Lusitania's *boilers*

would look after her. Alice Lines was too busy with Audrey and Stuart to have time to worry very much about what would happen. But her employer, Major Warren Pearl, told her carefully what to do if there was an attack. She must get the children out onto the open deck. He and his wife would come and find them there.

Captain Will Turner realized that his passengers were growing fearful, but he was still convinced that the *Lusitania* was too fast for any U-boat to catch. He knew a fact that some passengers were only just discovering for the first time—on this crossing, the ship's top speed was only twenty-one knots, not the twenty-five knots she had been designed to achieve. This was because the Cunard company had ordered one of the four boiler rooms to be shut down to save coal. But the captain thought this

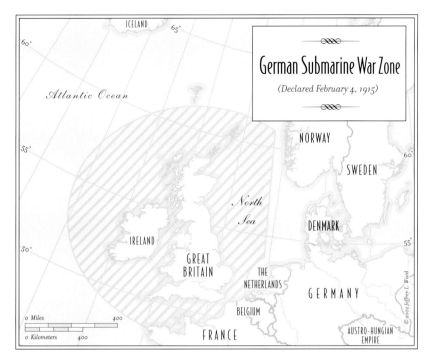

Map of German submarine war zone

did not matter. After all, no ship traveling at fifteen knots or more had ever been sunk by a U-boat.

Turner was confident that his engineers, six decks below, could easily produce enough speed to evade any attacking U-boat. Down in the scorching, acrid heat of the boiler rooms, the stokers would be rhythmically shoveling best-quality New England coal into the glowing furnaces. Protecting their faces, they would be raking the burning coals to produce the hottest fire to heat the water in the boilers to make steam. The steam then went hissing through the large pipes to the neighboring engine room, where it fed the gently throbbing turbine engines. The ringing of bells signaled orders from the bridge to reduce or increase power, and an engineer carefully adjusted the valves. In an emergency all of them—stokers and engineers—would carry out his orders skillfully and effectively.

The captain's confidence received a bit of a blow when, on the evening of Thursday, May 6, less than forty-eight hours before they were due in Liverpool, breathless bellboy Ben Holton handed him a brief message from the radio room. It was from the British Navy and read, "Submarines active off south coast of Ireland." Will Turner would have been even more concerned to know that during the six days the *Lusitania* had been at sea, German U-boats had sunk twenty-six ships in the very waters the *Lusitania* was about to enter. Some of them, of course, had been destroyed by the *U-20*.

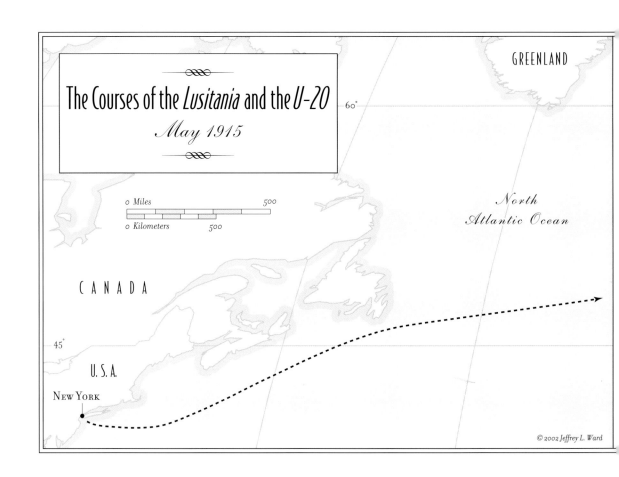

The Courses of the *Lusitania* and the *U-20*

May 1915

0 Miles · 500

0 Kilometers · 500

GREENLAND

North Atlantic Ocean

60°

CANADA

45°

U. S. A.

NEW YORK

© 2002 Jeffrey L. Ward

Turner had already taken some precautions. That morning Avis and others had wakened to the sound of bangs and shouts as the crewmen swung the lifeboats out over the side of the ship, ready to be lowered quickly in a crisis. The captain had also ordered his crew to put out all outside lights that night and to cover up cabin skylights and portholes. In addition he had doubled the number of seamen on lookout duty. Now he wondered what else he could do, but he knew he must soon get ready to attend the passenger talent concert taking place later that evening. It was a traditional event, and his passengers would think it was very odd if he were not there.

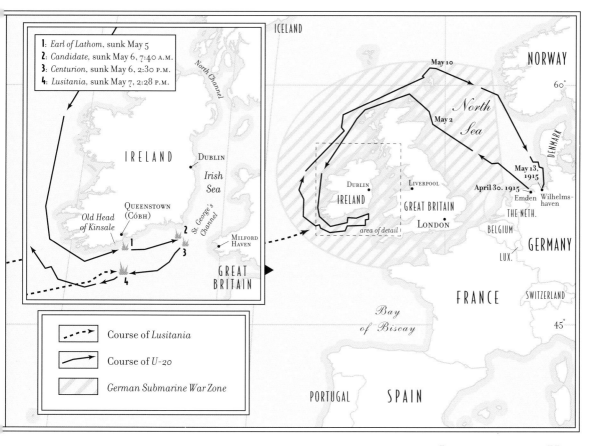

Map of the courses of the Lusitania *and the* U-20

Passengers taking their seats for the concert, however, were already noticing something unusual. Instead of the usual jolly atmosphere, people seemed subdued, sitting in quiet twos and threes. Still, some were making an effort to be cheerful and sociable. The concert was a way of raising money for seamens' charities. Millionaire Alfred Vanderbilt generously insisted on paying a young Canadian girl five dollars for one of the ten-cent, gold-embossed programs she was selling.

There were the usual songs, jokes, and magic tricks, but everything fell a bit flat. When the intermission came, there was an expectant hush as Captain Turner stepped forward to address his passengers. He explained that he had received a warning about submarines but assured them that "on entering the war zone tomorrow, we shall be securely in the care of the Royal Navy" and that there was no cause for alarm. He intended to steam at full speed through the danger zone. He also warned male passengers not to smoke on the open deck that night. A lurking U-boat could easily spot the glowing tip of a cigar or cigarette.

People were not reassured by what the captain had said. As soon as the concert had ended with "God Save the King" and "God Bless America," an anxious murmuring broke out. Some were so frightened that they decided not to go to their cabins but to sleep in one of the lounges. If the ship was attacked during the night, it would be easier to get out on deck and to the lifeboats from there. The thought of being trapped belowdecks was terrifying. Some even insisted on sleeping in their life jackets. Stewards and stewardesses were soon hurrying to and fro with blankets and pillows, trying to make everybody comfortable.

The Hooks, the Pearls, and Avis Dolphin were not among

those who camped out that night. They all went down to their cabins and tried to sleep, but it was hard to ignore the growing sense of menace. One little boy added to his prayers the plea, "Don't let the nasty submarines get us."

Passengers were not the only anxious ones. On the Scottish isle of Foula, Professor Ian Holbourn's wife, Marion, had a strange dream that night about "a large vessel sinking with a big list from side to side and also from stem to stern. There was a crush of frightened people, some of them slipping and sliding down the sloping decks." But there was nothing she or the passengers could do except wait and hope their fears had been wrong.

While passengers slept fitfully, the *Lusitania*'s seamen worked through the night. Lookouts were replaced every two hours, but it was stressful, eyestraining work peering anxiously into the dark and jumping at shadows. They could not know that out there, beneath the dark waters, the *U-20* was waiting, her crew also worried about what the next day would bring.

TORPEDOED

At 5:00 A.M. on Friday, May 7, Walther Schwieger surfaced to find thick fog, but by 10:00 A.M. visibility was good, and his lookouts spotted a small trawler sailing toward them. Suspecting that it might be a British naval patrol boat, Schwieger gave the order to dive. The *U-20* would not attack but would hide quietly beneath the waves until the trawler had passed. He did not want to risk revealing her presence when he had other, larger prey in mind.

Resurfacing at 1:20 P.M., he could hardly believe his eyes. There directly ahead was "a forest of masts and stacks." At first he thought that "they must belong to several ships. Then I saw it was a great steamer coming over the horizon." As he and his men watched in growing excitement, they made out the four great stacks of a large passenger steamer.

It was the moment for action. Schwieger yelled the order, "Alarm. *Tauchen!*" and his men hurled themselves down the steel ladder. Quick, efficient hands spun the wheels opening the vents to flood the *U-20*'s tanks with water while the boat's pumps expelled the air from them. The *U-20* slid under the water to a depth of thirty-five feet. Powered by her quiet electric motors, she began a stealthy approach as, all unsuspecting, the *Lusitania* sailed closer.

*U-boat officer
looking through a
periscope*

Schwieger watched anxiously through the lens of his periscope. Would he really be able to catch her? At first he thought his
efforts would be useless: "When the steamer was two miles away,
she changed her course. I had no hope now, even if we hurried at
our best speed, of getting near enough to attack her." But then "I
saw the steamer change her course again. She was coming directly
at us. She could not have steered a more perfect course if she had
deliberately tried to give us a dead shot." He changed the *U-20*'s
position just a little and waited patiently for his chance.

On board the *Lusitania*, the passengers were just finishing
their lunch. They were thankful that the night had passed without

incident, but that morning they had woken to the mournful sound of the ship's foghorn. Coming out on deck, they found the ship slowly probing her way through thick mist. It was worrisome. But as it began to clear, their fears and apprehensions evaporated, especially when land came in sight. Avis was thrilled to see a green smudge of land appearing off the ship's port bow, which Professor Holbourn told her was the southern coast of Ireland. The sight seemed to make everyone feel safer.

Flor and Julia Sullivan, a young couple who were also out on deck and scanning the coastline, were especially happy. Ireland was their home. They had met while Julia was working as house-keeper to an elderly couple on Long Island. Flor needed work, and, so that the couple could afford to marry, Julia's kind employers had found him a job as a bartender in New York, which he loved. But now they were returning to Ireland to take over the Sullivan family farm.

Still, as the morning wore on, the Sullivans, like many passengers, were surprised that the *Lusitania* was still going so slowly now that the fog had lifted. It seemed to be asking for trouble. Frank and Elsie Hook, running along the decks, passed groups of puzzled passengers wondering what could be the cause. Was Captain Turner waiting for a British Royal Navy escort to convoy the *Lusitania* safely into Liverpool? Or perhaps the ship had been damaged, sabotaged even? Maybe the three German stowaways had managed to inflict some harm on her before they were caught?

But the truth was none of those things. Captain Turner had decided to reduce speed so that he could time the *Lusitania*'s arrival off Liverpool to coincide with high tide the next morning. This would allow the *Lusitania* to sail straight over the sandbank known as the Mersey Bar, which at low tide blocked the entrance to the Mersey River leading up to Liverpool and safety. If he arrived at the Mersey Bar when the tides were low, he would have to wait, which would be highly dangerous, since German U-boats often lurked around the approaches to Liverpool.

Photo of a U-boat torpedo room

Also, the thick fog earlier that morning had made it difficult for Captain Turner to be sure exactly where his ship was. Careful navigator that he was, he asked one of his officers to calculate her position by measuring how far she was from various points along the Irish coast. This was a complicated task during which the ship had to be held steady and sail in a straight line, and this too was slowing her down.

As the young officer was carefully taking his measurements, Walther Schwieger closed in for the kill. When the *Lusitania* was just over seven hundred yards away, he ordered his torpedo officer, Raimund Weisbach, to prepare to fire. At 2:10 P.M. Schwieger gave the order. With a shudder and a hiss, the heavy torpedo went singing through the water, unleashing a trail of bubbles. It was longer and heavier than an automobile, and as wide and round as a steering wheel.

The lookout on the *Lusitania*'s starboard side, eighteen-year-old seaman Leslie Morton, was horrified to see "a turmoil and what looked like a bubble on a large scale in the water." Grabbing a megaphone, he yelled, "Torpedoes coming on the starboard side, sir." His next thought was that he must warn his brother John, who was also a seaman on board and who was resting below. So he hur-

Eye-witness sketch of the torpedo's impact, by ship passenger Oliver Bernard

ried to find him. The other lookouts were now shouting to the bridge. Captain Turner heard the frantic cries and came running on to the bridge, but it was too late to take evasive action. He heard a sound "like the banging of a door on a windy day" followed by "a kind of rumble," as he later recalled. The *Lusitania* had been hit.

Turner ordered his helmsman to steer hard for the shore. The man swung the wheel, but the ship would not respond. The steering mechanism had locked. The despairing captain tried to slow the ship by putting the engines into reverse, but they would not respond either. Will Turner had to face the fact that the *Lusitania* was out of control, swinging helplessly out to sea. He ordered his officers to launch the lifeboats.

Passengers walking on deck had also seen the torpedo come speeding toward the ship. They had felt the ship shudder at the

Inside the image:
FUNNEL DAMAGE
BOAT DECK
PROMENADE DECK
SHELTER DECK
Dotted line → represents approximate height of water & debris thrown up by the explosion
Approximate size of vast hole caused by Torpedo
Torpedo
← Area affected (Rivets started Etc) →

*Diagram of where
the torpedo hit*

moment she was hit. Water, coal, and debris shot into the sky and then rained down on the deck. Then, within seconds, came a second rumbling explosion. Within moments the ship was tilting alarmingly to starboard.

Water began pouring in great green waves through the lower decks, which were in total darkness because the electricity had failed. Up in the radio room on the top deck, radio officer Bob Leith had to switch to emergency power supplies as he tapped out an urgent SOS message over and over again: LUSITANIA. COME AT ONCE, BIG LIST OFF SOUTH HEAD, OLD KINSALE.

Frantic officers, running to their places at the lifeboats, shouted at passengers not to panic—but few listened. They were already crowding the stairways, pushing and shoving and shouting. They were desperate to reach the open air and the lifeboats on the upper decks and to find their families. Professor Holbourn guessed that Avis would still be in the second-class dining room. He waited until the worst rush was over, then fought his way against the tide of frightened people to find her.

He was right. Avis was in the dining room. She had been enjoying her last delicious lunch before she got to Liverpool and was looking forward to a dessert of pears and blancmange when she felt the whole ship shaken by a tremendous blow. Now she was sitting alone and terrified among the spilled food, smashed crockery, and shattered glass, wondering what to do. The professor ran quickly to her. He knew that time was running out. The ship was leaning over at such an alarming rate she couldn't last long. They needed life jackets, and quickly.

Taking Avis firmly by the hand, he pushed his way back to the staircase. The tilting ship made it hard to climb. Sometimes they had to put one foot on the side wall, not the steps, because the ship was tipping over so much. Beside them shrieking people clutched at each other, scrambling, slipping, and falling. Reaching his stateroom at last, high up on the Boat Deck, Holbourn searched for a spare life jacket on top of the closet. He found one at last, pulled it over Avis's head, and tied the white tapes carefully and securely around her so that it could not slip.

Then he told her to stay there while he went to look for her nurse, Hilda Ellis. Avis bravely waited alone in the tilting cabin, trying not to listen to the shouting, banging, and running feet out in the passageway. By a miracle the professor found the frightened nurse in the surging crowd. As they rushed back to Avis, he offered

Drawing of Lusitania *passengers struggling in the water*

her his own life jacket. Hilda refused it, insisting that he had a wife and three children and must rescue himself. They compromised—if he could find her a place in a lifeboat, he would keep the jacket.

The professor led Avis and Hilda out of the cabin on to the crowded, sloping decks. It was chaos. People were swarming over the port side of the ship, the highest from the water, hoping to get into the lifeboats. But because the ship was leaning over on her side, the heavy wooden boats were swinging in over the deck. It was almost impossible to lower them so that people could climb in. A big burly passenger with a black beard pulled out a revolver and waved it in the face of two crewmen who stood hesitating by one of the lifeboats. "Don't you see the ship is sinking?" he yelled at them. "The first man that disobeys my orders to launch the boat, I shoot to kill." The seamen struggled to lower the boat, but it fell from its ropes and came crashing down the deck, crushing people in its path.

Injured and bleeding people littered the deck. Horrified, Professor Holbourn decided their best chance was on the lower starboard side. He forced a way through crowds that were stumbling and sliding over the deck. Baby carriages rolled about wildly, their tiny occupants crying helplessly. No one could stand up without hanging on to the ship's rail. Terrified people clutched at the rail and each other to stop themselves from falling into the water. One young girl fell and rolled the full length of the deck before being picked up by a steward. Another woman remembered that the tilt was so severe that "we had to sort of rush down, clinging to the railing, which at that time was nearly underwater . . . and sort of tumble into the boat, assisted by passengers and seamen."

At last Professor Holbourn managed to reach a starboard boat. He braced his strong body against the crowd and lifted Avis and Hilda across the gap into the swaying boat. As he did so, he kissed Avis good-bye. Already water was pouring over the bow of the ship. In minutes she would be gone. The professor, believing he was going to die, asked Avis calmly and gently "to find his wife and children and kiss them good-bye from him" when she reached Britain. He watched as her lifeboat was lowered away. Then, pulling out his pocket watch from his tweed jacket, he was

shocked to see that it had only been twelve minutes since the torpedo had hit the *Lusitania*.

Hurriedly but carefully, Holbourn put on the life jacket he was still carrying and slithered forward to find a section of ship's rail that was clear of passengers. His only chance was to jump. He climbed onto the rail, but as he leaped from it into the blue-green waters below, he had the horrible shock of seeing Avis's boat swamp and capsize as two men jumped into it. For a moment he saw Avis flailing about. He started swimming through the cold water but could not reach her through the mass of wreckage and people gasping for breath around him. He could only watch in despair as the water, swirling against the ship's side, pulled her under, and she disappeared beneath the waves.

Frank and Elsie Hook and their father, George, managed to keep together as they struggled up from the third-class dining room out into the open air to try and find a place in a lifeboat. Seeing the crush and the confusion on deck around the lifeboats, George told his children they had no chance of getting to them. The ship was sinking quickly, and they had no choice but to jump for their lives from the rail. At that moment Elsie saw a wad of dollar bills lying on the deck. As she darted forward to grab it, her father told her to leave it alone. What mattered was not money but saving their lives. Nervously they climbed up and over the wooden bar and, holding hands, leaped into the cold, churning waters of the sea below.

THE LAST MINUTES

George Hook had been right. Time was fast running out for those still on board. For a moment the ship had seemed to straighten herself in a rocking motion. Then almost at once came the sensation that she was leaning even more heavily to starboard, tilting over and over. At the same time the *Lusitania* was sinking headfirst. Water surged over her bow as it dipped beneath the waves.

Julia Sullivan's husband, Flor, found places in a lifeboat for both of them, but seeing what was happening to the lifeboats, Julia decided their best bet was to jump overboard. Even though Flor could not swim, Julia was a strong swimmer, and she was sure she could save them both. She tucked their money into her dress, chose a place to jump from, and told Flor to hold on tight to her. Lovers Gerda Nielson and Jack Welsh, who had decided just the night

Drawing of the sequence of the sinking

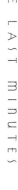

before to marry as soon as they reached England, also decided to leap into the water together.

But many were too confused or too afraid either to try to get to a lifeboat or to jump. Instead they were running around aimlessly, panic-stricken. Among them was a stoker who had been injured in one of the explosions in the boiler rooms. Sixteen-year-old cook George Wynne, who had been working on a mountain of vegetables for that night's dinner when the torpedo hit, was amazed by the chaos when he reached the open decks with his father, Joseph, who was also a cook. His father told him to stay where he was while he rushed off to find him a life jacket. But time passed, and his father did not return. Another man pushed George toward the rail, telling him it was no use waiting. George hesitated, then jumped over the side. Somebody pulled him into a lifeboat, where he sat trembling in his thin cook's white jacket and checked trousers. Looking anxiously back at the ship, he could see no sign of his father.

A number of people were heroically trying to help others, even if it meant sacrificing their own lives. Stewards and stewardesses struggled along pitch-black passageways flooded with water to make sure no one was still in the cabins. Alfred Vanderbilt, who could not swim, although he owned one of the most beautiful swimming pools in America, gave his life jacket to a frightened woman and helped her put it on, tying the tapes tight for her. Then, realizing how many children had become separated from their parents and were wandering helpless and lost, he told his valet, Ronald Denyer, "to find all the kiddies you can." As brave as his employer, Ronald brought them to Vanderbilt, who ran to the boats with a child in each arm time and time again. A

*Reconstruction of
the sinking*

witness thought that Vanderbilt looked as calm as if he were waiting for a train.

The *Lusitania*'s bow was quickly submerging, and as she tipped
forward, her huge propellers and rudder were rising up out of the
water. These were her dying moments. Children were now being
thrown from the decks, to be caught by men in the lifeboats on
the sea below. One young man was startled to find two babies snug-
gled in the shelter of a deck house. As the ship neared her final
plunge, he tucked one under each arm and took a flying leap over
the side.

But for some there was no escape. When the torpedo first hit
the ship, a group of butchers were hard at work belowdecks on the

Elevators in first class

meat for that evening's dinner. They jumped into the electric elevator used to bring the meat up and down, only to be trapped when the ship's electricity failed. A young bellboy was horrified by their screams and by the knowledge that "they knew they were trapped." The passenger elevators had also stopped. They were caught between two floors, and the people inside could only beat futilely on the elegant metal grilles that had become their cage.

The three German stowaways, locked in their cell belowdecks, were also trapped. They heard the explosions, the shouts, the sound of people crashing about in the dark. Then came the sound of rushing water. They must have wondered frantically and despairingly whether anyone would remember they were there. Even if they did, no one ever reached them.

Alice Lines had been much luckier. She was belowdecks when the torpedo hit the ship. Instinctively she rushed to find baby Audrey and little Stuart. With trembling fingers she tied Audrey tightly in a woolen shawl around her neck, grabbed hold of Stuart, "and took them up on deck as quick as possible." The slender young woman recalled she found it hard struggling with "a baby in her arms and a little boy of five hanging to her skirt."

She managed to reach a lifeboat. A grim-faced crewman scooped up Stuart and lifted the little boy across the gap between the rail and the lifeboat. But when Alice tried to follow Stuart across into the boat, the sailor told her firmly it was full. What was she to do? She could not let Stuart go alone, and she must save Audrey. As the lifeboat was lowered, the distraught girl decided she had to jump. Cradling Audrey as best as she could, she held her breath and leaped. Alice landed in the water beside the lifeboat and for a moment had "a terrible sensation of being sucked under the ship." But then she felt someone grab her long auburn hair and pull her on board, still clutching the baby. As she later said, "My hair saved our lives!"

Alice's lifeboat was one of the very few to get safely away. The *Lusitania* was now tilting at such an angle and the ship was sinking with such speed that launching the boats became almost impossible. On the port side, boats swinging inward smashed against the ship's side. Men fought to push them out over the ship's rail so they could be lowered, but the boats were too heavy, and the

Alice Lines

mass of people crowding around and trying to get in obstructed them. A few boats were successfully swung over the rail, but as they were lowered, they scraped against the giant rivets sticking out from the ship's side and were ripped apart.

On the starboard side the boats were swinging so far out that people had to leap across a huge gap to board them. Many were too frightened to jump the seven or eight feet into the boats. In any case it was very hard to lower the crowded boats. Seamen, including Leslie Morton and his brother, John, struggled to hold the ropes steady so the boats could descend evenly. But some tipped, spilling their human cargo into the sea below. Others capsized when they hit the water. Bellboy Ben Holton also tried to help launch the boats, but gave up in despair. He slipped through a mass of pushing and struggling people, hopped on the ship's rail,

Eyewitness sketch of smokestacks going under, by Oliver Bernard

and dove into the Atlantic.

As Alice sat shuddering with cold and shock, wondering what had happened to the rest of the Pearl family, two seamen rowed her lifeboat hurriedly away from the sinking ship so it wouldn't be sucked down with her. The *Lusitania*'s huge smokestacks loomed over the lifeboat, casting dark shadows.

All around, people were now dropping into the water. One man jumped from the stern, only to have his leg sliced off by a propeller. The masts were covered with people climbing ever higher, still refusing to let go. Then, with a long, lingering moan, the "big Lusy" made her final plunge, disappearing beneath the waves. Just eighteen frantic minutes after the *U-20* had launched her torpedo, the liner was gone.

Walther Schwieger watched the disaster he had created through his periscope. He had been very, very lucky. It had taken thirty-five seconds for his torpedo to reach the *Lusitania*. During that time the ship had traveled nearly one and a half times her own length. If he had launched the torpedo just five seconds earlier or twenty seconds later, he would have missed his target altogether instead of hitting it in one of the places where it could do the most damage.

But now his mind must have been on the human drama unfolding before him. He later told a friend, "It was the most terrible sight I have ever seen. It was impossible for me to give any help. I could have saved only

Oliver Bernard,
survivor and artist

a handful. The scene was too horrible to watch, and I gave orders to dive to twenty meters and away." But as the *U-20* turned for home, the struggle was far from over for those he was leaving behind.

Depiction of passengers struggling

The people splashing about in the water or sitting shivering in lifeboats were seeing some terrifying sights. As cold seawater had poured down the smokestacks of the sinking ship, a number of people had been sucked deep inside. Then, suddenly, when the ship's boilers exploded, they were shot out again like human cannonballs, covered in soot and oil. One of them, a vicar's wife, had had her clothes entirely ripped off. These survivors looked barely human, but they were still alive. Eager hands pulled them into a lifeboat.

The survivors looked numbly around them. Nothing was left but an ever-widening circle of debris and floating bodies—some alive and some dead. Many people had drowned because they had put their life jackets on upside down. Their heads were underwater, and their legs were sticking pathetically into the air. Others had not tied their jackets on tightly enough, so that they had come off and were now bobbing beside them in the water. Survivors clung to anything that was floating—packing cases, dog kennels, even the remains of a grand piano.

Some people had tied their children to chairs in the hope they would float. Now they drifted helplessly about in the water, calling out for their parents. Nine-year-old Edith Williams, separated from her mother, Annie, and five brothers and sisters, was saved by a young woman who saw her being swept away and managed to

Edith and Edward Williams as children

grab her skirt. Avis Dolphin had survived being thrown from the lifeboat and sucked down into the sea. She managed to fight her way up through the dark water to the light above, choking and spluttering as she surfaced. She owed her life to the fact that the professor had tied her life jacket on correctly, and it had helped push her back up. Eventually the shivering girl was pulled out of the water by a man floating alone in one of the collapsible lifeboats.

Unknown to Avis, the professor was in the cold water and now in far more danger than she. He was hoping that a lifeboat would come to his rescue. But many boats were full to their capacity, and the people inside were terrified of taking on more people and capsizing. Some were even rapping the knuckles of those clinging to the sides to make them drop off.

The professor swam toward the nearest boat he could see, trying to help a man floating alongside him by pushing him along. When he reached the boat, he was shocked to discover his companion was dead. Even more shocking was the fact that the people in the boat refused to take him aboard in case the extra weight sank it. Teeth chattering with cold, the desperate Holbourn grabbed a rope trailing from the boat's stern and hung grimly on.

The people in the boat now spotted another empty one a few yards away and began to row toward it, but their progress was agonizingly slow. The professor knew he could not last much longer. Each time he asked how much farther it was, he was told to hang on another five minutes. The exhausted man begged someone in the boat to help him by holding his hand, but they all

refused on the grounds that it would be "uncomfortable."
At last he was dragged into the second boat, where he
sat trying to shut his eyes and ears to "the sight and
sound of the people drowning all around."

Gerda Nielson was also shocked by people's
selfishness. After she and Jack had jumped into the
sea, Jack had supported her in the water until she
was picked up by a lifeboat. But she had to plead with
her rescuers, who were insisting their boat was full, before
they eventually pulled Jack in as well.

Kathleen Kaye

Still, many passengers and crew were doing their best to help
each other. Bookseller Charles Lauriat from Boston and two
other men spotted an empty collapsible boat and managed to
climb onto it and raise the canvas sides. Then they rowed about,
picking up more and more grateful people, until the boat was so
low in the water it was almost sinking. Even then Lauriat felt it
was impossible to refuse to help people. Hearing a man cry out to
him, he decided, "You couldn't go off and leave that one more
soul floating around," and he picked him up. Fourteen-year-old
Kathleen Kaye, who had been traveling home to England after a
visit to New York, took the oar of another boat and rowed tire-
lessly. When not rowing, she helped people into the boat, gave
first aid to the wounded, and kept up people's spirits with her
cheerful courage.

Elizabeth Duckworth, the weaver from Taftville befriended
by the Hooks, was another hero. She was sitting in a lifeboat, so
overcome by all the terrible sights that she was reciting the
Twenty-third Psalm, when she saw a man "struggling in the water
right near our boat, and I said to the mate: 'Can't we help him?'

Bob Leith

He said, 'No.' I said, 'Yes, we can.'" After "a very hard struggle" they managed to pull him in. In fact, all around, small selfless acts of kindness and humanity were saving lives. A half-drowned woman with a two-inch gash to her head and cuts all over her back, dressed only in a thin petticoat and blouse, was pulled from the sea and determinedly began giving artificial respiration to two people.

But as minutes turned to hours, the survivors scanned the horizon with increasing desperation. They could see land, but where were the rescue boats? The horizon was empty. The blinding sunlight dancing over the sparkling waters added to the torment. Many were choking for a drink of water, their tongues swollen. Even though it was a fine day, the sea was cold—52 degrees Fahrenheit. Many were dying of cold. The sea was dotted with dead and dying.

But help was coming. Radio officer Bob Leith's SOS message had been picked up in Queenstown. A fleet of rescue boats from naval vessels to fishing boats to lifeboats had been dispatched, but Queenstown was twenty-five miles away. Elsewhere along the coast, people had actually seen the *Lusitania* go down. These included the coxswain of the lifeboat stationed at Courtmacsherry, a village south of Queenstown. He rushed to the lifeboat station, fired the signal calling the crew, and within three minutes the crew were aboard. But with no engine, it would take them some three hours to reach the scene. They prayed as they rowed, "As hard as men could pray. O God, keep them alive until we're there."

Bo529

3 1000 pads 12/14va G & S 754

COPY OF TELEGRAM.

IN

From

    Corkbeg WSS

DATE **7.5.15**

SENT **2.30 pm**

To— Admiralty.

RECD. **3.3 pm**

D.70 61 message 7th 2.25 pm.

     S.O.S. from LUSITANIA. We think we are off Kinsale.
late position 10 miles off Kinsale come at once big list
later please come with all haste.

Circulated to :-

1st L.

1st S.L.

Sir A.Wilson.

D.C.2

D.I.D.

Trade.

S.A.C.

C.C.

CHAPTER SEVEN

RESCUERS AND SURVIVORS

American Wesley Frost was working quietly in his office in Queenstown. It was his job, as U.S. consul, to give help and advice to American citizens in Ireland. Sometimes liners like the *Lusitania* stopped at Queenstown on their way to England, and American passengers would come to see him. They would ask him about the progress of the war and which places it was safe for them to visit in Europe.

Suddenly Frost's colleague, Vice Consul Lewis Thompson, burst into the room. He said there was "a wildfire rumor about town that the *Lusitania* had been attacked." The two men hurried over to the window and saw an unusual commotion. About two dozen tugs and fishing boats were steaming toward the harbor mouth. Frost grabbed the phone and called the British Navy office. "It's true," a young officer told him, "we fear she has gone."

Frost knew that many Americans had been on board the ship. He immediately went to the bank to withdraw money to help survivors. Then, with a heavy heart, he sent a cable to the U.S. government in Washington: LUSITANIA SUNK 2:30 TODAY . . . RESCUE WORK ENERGETICALLY PROCEEDING SHALL I CABLE LIST OF SURVIVORS.

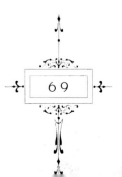

Map/drawing of how Irish boats came to the aid of the Lusitania *passengers*

Cries of "The Lusy's gone!" were soon echoing around the town. Hotel owners and their guests busied themselves getting rooms ready for the shipwrecked passengers. At their offices down on the harbor, shocked Cunard officials cabled the unbelievable news to their head office in Liverpool. Everyone knew that the worst thing now would be the waiting. None of the rescue vessels had radios. There could be no news until they returned, and that would not be for several hours. Nevertheless people were already clustering expectantly by the wooden Cunard wharf.

The fishing boat *Peel 12* was the first to reach the scene of the disaster. She had been fishing for mackerel when her crew had seen the *Lusitania* sinking about three miles away. Elizabeth Duckworth, still rowing hard, was in one of the first lifeboats that the *Peel 12* found. She helped the battered, exhausted people climb out of the lifeboat into the fishing boat and was about to follow them. Then she spotted another lifeboat "tossing about in the water" with only three people in it. One of the three stood up and begged for help to go back and rescue some of the drowning. The captain of the *Peel 12* refused, saying he could not spare the men. Elizabeth was disgusted and at once leapt into the lifeboat. Together with her three male companions, she rowed off and rescued "about forty of those struggling in the water." The admiring fishermen cheered her as she returned with her boatload of grateful, shivering people.

But the crew of the *Peel 12* were horrified by the survivors' condition. Many were badly injured and bleeding. Some were naked, and their teeth were chattering with cold. Crewmen rushed to find bandages, to pull the blankets from their bunks, and to brew hot tea. Among those sitting huddled and dripping in the boat's tiny hold, which smelled strongly of fish, was Professor Holbourn. Next to him lay a man with a broken leg. A woman was moaning, "Why didn't they come before?"

More and more rescue boats were arriving now. Unknown to Professor Holbourn, Avis was safe on board one of them. Wrapped in a blanket and with a hot drink in her hands, she was huddling near the stove for warmth. She was touched to see a little boy suddenly reunited with his parents, who thought he had drowned. George Hook and his daughter, Elsie, were also rescued, but had no idea what had happened to young Frank. After jumping into the sea, they had lost sight of him amid all the wreckage.

The New York Times
reports the sinking

It was sometimes hard for the rescuers to know who was still alive and who was dead as they pulled the bodies on board. Bellboy Ben Holton had passed out from the cold as he floated on a piece of wreckage to which some unknown person had tied him. He woke to find himself laid out on a ship's hatch among a pile of dead bodies. He was very weak but managed to sit up, startling a sailor who exclaimed, "Good gracious, are you alive? We put you among the dead ones." He helped Ben cut off his soaking life jacket and gave him a cup of strong coffee. The fashionably dressed woman with the straw hat and pointed nose who had complained about her cabin was also dragged seemingly lifeless on board a rescue boat. The sailors were convinced she was dead, but another woman insisted they try to revive her. To their amazement, her eyelids flickered, and she mumbled a few words. They hurried her to a warm stove.

Major Warren Pearl was rescued by the steamer *Katrina,* but he had no idea what had happened to his wife and children. Captain Will Turner was on board the trawler *Bluebell.* He had been washed off the bridge of the *Lusitania* as she went under and had survived by clinging to some wreckage. One of the *Lusitania*'s seamen had spotted the sun glinting on the gold braid of his uniform and had managed to pull him out of the water. Now he was sitting by the stove wrapped in a blanket, thinking about the terrible thing that had happened to his ship.

As the boats filled up, they turned for Queenstown or for the little fishing town of Kinsale, which was nearer. The journey seemed endless. People were in a state of shock, finding it hard to believe what had happened to them. Many had swollen tongues and throats that were raw from swallowing seawater. Some of the rescue boats did not have enough freshwater on board for them to drink. A few were looking anxiously out to sea, terrified that German submarines were perhaps still lurking, waiting to attack the rescue fleet.

The Courtmacsherry lifeboat, whose men had rowed until, as one later described, their "hearts were well-nigh broken," arrived too late to save the living. All they saw were bodies floating in the sea. In the dusk they thought they saw someone trying to signal to them with a torch. They rowed eagerly over, only to find that the light was coming from the last rays of the sun catching on the diamond ring of a dead woman. Sadly the exhausted, disappointed men began the slow journey home.

Consul Frost, waiting anxiously at the Cunard wharf, saw the first rescue boats come in out of the darkness with their cargoes of "the living and the dead." The wharf was lit by gas torches, and as he watched, "bruised and shuddering women, crippled and half-clothed men, and a few wide-eyed little children" were helped or carried up the gangplank. Anyone feeling strong enough was led into the brightly lit Cunard offices to register his or her name. Next the survivors went to the specially opened Queenstown post office to wire their families that they were safe. Young cook George Wynne sent a telegram to his mother in Liverpool telling her that he and his father, Joseph, were safe. The sad truth, though, was different. He had no idea what had happened to Joseph, but he could not bear the thought of his mother worrying.

Woman rescued from the Lusitania, *May 25, 1915*

(Information on) survivor-wanted poster

Afterward, George and the others were taken to hotels, lodging houses, and private homes where women wrapped them in blankets, dosed them with brandy, and put them to bed with hot-water bottles. Elizabeth Duckworth, suffering from cold, exhaustion, and shock, was relieved to be able to lie down in safety at last in the little Westbourne Hotel.

Some could find no rest. A woman with a baby in her arms stood by the wharf and scanned the face of every survivor who came ashore in the vain hope of finding her husband. Alice Lines, still clutching Audrey and little Stuart, was worrying about the rest of the Pearls. What had happened to Major and Mrs. Pearl, and to nurse Greta Lorenson and little Amy and Susan? People found it hard to sleep that night, wondering what had become of friends and family and jumping at every knock on the door. Professor Holbourn, waiting anxiously in his hotel for news of Avis, was hugely relieved when a message was brought to him at around 2:00 A.M. that she was safe. She was, in fact, sitting up in bed in the same hotel, sipping a glass of hot milk.

Early the next morning survivors began walking the streets of Queenstown, hoping to find their loved ones. Some parents, separated from their children in the frantic scramble on the sinking ship and desperate for news, placed advertisements in local newspapers and shop windows. One notice read,

> Lusitania—*missing a baby girl, 15 months old. Very fair curly hair and rosy complexion. In white woolen jersey and white woolen leggings. Tries to walk and talk. Name Betty Bretherton. Please send any information to Miss Browne, Queen's House, Queenstown.*

George Hook and his daughter, Elsie, toured the temporary morgues that had hastily been opened. The scenes inside were terrible. They saw a heap of what looked like battered, bruised, broken dolls rather than people. To their great relief, there was no sign of Frank. Then came news that Frank was in a Queenstown hospital, and they rushed to his bedside. Frank, overcome with relief and happiness because he had assumed they were both dead, told them what had happened. His leg had been broken by a falling lifeboat. He had fainted but had been rescued and carried ashore, unconscious. The doctors explained to George that it would take a long time for Frank to recover. In fact, he would be the last *Lusitania* survivor to be discharged from the hospital.

There were other happy reunions. Flor and Julia Sullivan had been torn apart when they jumped into the water. Flor had been rescued and taken to Queenstown. Julia had been brought to

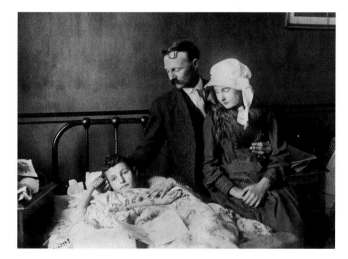

Frank Hook and family in the hospital

Kinsale, where she was taken straight to a hospital, suffering from cold, exhaustion, and shock. But the day after the sinking, a priest who had visited her managed to find Flor and tell him the wonderful news that his wife was alive. Leslie and John Morton, who had dived into the water as the ship made her final plunge, had each believed the other was dead. The two seamen were miserably wandering the streets of Queenstown when they suddenly ran into each other. The delighted brothers went off to celebrate at a pub.

Lucy Taylor, the young bride whose new peacock-feathered hat had been hurled into the Hudson River by a sailor as the *Lusitania* left New York, was also lucky. Although she had refused to be parted from her husband, Harold, screaming, "I won't go, I won't!" as she struggled to stay upright on the wildly tilting deck, he had picked her up and dropped her into a lifeboat. As the lifeboat pulled away, she had seen him waving "as he went down with the boat." She was convinced he was dead. But that morning, as she came sadly down the steps of her hotel, a man in sailor's clothes ran up to her. For a moment she did not recognize him. Then she saw it was Harold.

Major Pearl, touring the town in despair, at last discovered that his wife was alive, but there was no news yet of their four children and the two nurses. Then he heard that a young woman answering Alice Lines's description had been taken in by local people. The anxious father rushed to the house to find Alice safe with baby Audrey and little Stuart. Greta Lorenson and his two daughters, Amy and Susan, though, were still missing. The major and Alice Lines did everything they could think of. They went again and again to the railway station, hoping that Greta and the girls had been rescued somewhere else along the coast and would take the train to Queenstown. But there was no news.

Meanwhile, dazed and confused survivors were wandering the town, ragged as scarecrows. Cunard officials gave them money so that they could buy themselves new clothes. The townspeople generously donated what they could. One woman had no clothes at all and had to sit wrapped in a blanket in her hotel room while a local woman went shopping for her. Soldiers lent their army greatcoats to two shivering young women who promised to mail them

Lusitania *survivor with injured hands, May 25, 1915*

back when they reached home. A broken Captain Turner walked the streets in his now shrunken, sea-stained uniform before deciding to go into a shop to buy himself a new hat.

Many were too ill to get out of bed, already showing symptoms of pneumonia and pleurisy. But some survivors who felt fit enough and only had themselves to think about were already preparing to leave Queenstown, anxious to leave this "town of the dead." The first departed the very day after the sinking, but it took courage to walk up the gangway onto a ship to cross the Irish Sea to Britain so soon after being torpedoed. Some people sat up all night on the ferry, still wearing their life jackets from the *Lusitania,* terrified of hearing the cry "Submarine!"

Captain Will Turner in his shrunken uniform

*Surviving crewmen
in Queenstown*

A number of the *Lusitania*'s crew-men were among the first to arrive at the ferry port of Holyhead. Together, many of them caught the first train to Liverpool. Crowds, sometimes hushed, sometimes hysterical, had been keeping vigil outside the Cunard company headquarters. Pale-faced officials were pasting up bulletins with the latest news. As one newspaper reported, each time a new name appeared on the list of survivors, "a piercing cry was heard, 'He's saved,' and three or four women would rush frantically away exclaiming 'Saved! Saved! Saved!'"

As the first trains carrying survivors drew into Liverpool's Lime Street railroad station, crowds surged up the platforms toward them. The train doors opened, and weary processions of men and women began filing off. Some were bandaged. Some were limping. A reporter noticed, "Not all of them had recovered from their daze and stupor." One man was still clutching his life jacket. When his friend tried to take it from him, he held fiercely on to it.

Sixteen-year-old cook George Wynne shrank back from the stampeding people. He knew that his mother would be somewhere in the crowd, with her new baby in her arms, but he was afraid to face her. It was only many hours later and with the help of a priest that George at last found the strength to go home and confess to his mother that his father had probably been drowned.

Professor Ian Holbourn cabled his wife, Marion, on the isle of Foula to say that he was safe and that he was taking "child Dolphin" to her grandparents in England. He suggested Marion should travel the long distance to join them. She had not learned of the sinking until the evening of the day it happened. An unthinking neighbor had called out, "Have you heard the news? The *Lusitania*'s down." Marion felt blackness surge toward her and had to hang on to the furniture so that she did not fall. She could not sleep that night and thought back to her strange dream of the night before. She got up early, dressed quickly, and went out to buy an early edition of that morning's newspaper. Her heart sank at the headline, VERY FEW SURVIVORS. Then a telegram boy brought the news that her husband had been rescued. She told her sons what had happened, and they ran around the house shouting, "The whole world is in an uproar! The *Lusitania*'s down, and my daddy's saved."

Man with life jacket

The Holbourns were lucky. Elsewhere, families were still anxiously waiting for news. Hundreds of people were still missing.

CHAPTER EIGHT

FOREVER CHANGED

While the wider world reeled with shock that the famous *Lusitania*, with so many people on board, had been sunk, the work of searching for survivors along the Irish coast continued. Even some of those who had themselves been rescued set off along the shore. They searched the coves and inlets, slithering over mounds of seaweed, in their quest for missing friends and family.

Soon, though, it became clear that there would be no more survivors. The coffins of some American victims were draped with Old Glory and sent home to the United States. Many victims, however, were buried locally. Some were unidentifiable. Some families couldn't afford the cost of bringing their loved ones home. Others thought it fitting to lay family members to rest near where the tragedy had taken place. On Monday, May 10, three days after the sinking, a funeral procession wound its way through the streets of Queenstown, up the hill past St. Colman's Cathedral to the Old Church Cemetery, two miles outside the town. A military band played a somber funeral march. The townspeople stood silent and

American victim of the Lusitania, *May 1915*

bareheaded along the streets. Flags on buildings and on ships in the harbor flew at half-mast. Mourners sang "Abide with Me" as coffins were lowered into the graves. A firing party loosed a volley of shots and twenty buglers sounded "The Last Post." In nearby Kinsale, where other victims were being buried, women lined the graves with moss and flowers.

Many bodies were never found. These included the body of Alfred Vanderbilt, who bravely sacrificed himself to save the lives of the children on board. His family offered a reward of $1,000 and people scoured the coastline of southern Ireland. His grieving mother sat in her huge mansion in New York, hoping against hope

Mass burial

for news that Alfred had perhaps been discovered alive in some remote part of Ireland, but it was futile. No news ever came.

Professor Holbourn quickly recovered his strength and was soon journeying with Avis to England. Marion Holbourn had guessed that her husband must have lost all his possessions, so she packed everything she thought he might need before setting out on her 450-mile journey to meet them at the Birmingham railroad station in England. But what, she wondered, could she bring to help "child Dolphin"? She had no idea how old she was. After joyfully greeting her husband at the station, Marion turned to see "a well-grown young lady of twelve years." She was surprised to see that the shyly smiling girl was not at all the infant she had imagined "child Dolphin" to be.

The professor was carrying some of his still-wet clothes over his arm. Mrs. Holbourn took the soggy garments from him and hurried off to find the trunk she had brought and pack them away. She explained to a puzzled porter who was watching her, "I've been meeting my husband. . . . He was on the *Lusitania*." Seeing the wet garments, the man replied, "O-oh, was he drowned then?"

The Holbourns took Avis to her grandparents' house near Worcester. Her grandfather was a man with large serious eyes and a long white beard. Marion was amazed when he told her that he had had an almost identical vision to hers the night before the sinking. He had seen a great ship go down and a little girl rise to the surface and had said to his wife, "Depend upon it, that's our Avis!"

Avis herself had recovered very quickly from her frightening experience. She had already written a long letter home, beginning, "My dearest Mother, I hope you are well. I am just splendid. I will tell you everything from the time we got on the boat until now." She told her mother all about the professor and how he had saved her life.

In fact, Avis later went to live with the Holbourns, and she and the professor remained close friends until he died in 1933. He even wrote an adventure story for her, *The Child of the Moat*, because she complained that stories written for girls were so dull.

The events of May 7, 1915, also forged deep bonds between nurse Alice Lines and the baby she saved, Audrey Pearl. They stayed in close touch throughout their lives, and in 1994 Alice, now a frail old lady, with her once-long auburn hair now white and cut short, told the *National Geographic* that Audrey was "still my baby." Alice died in 1997 at age one hundred. Audrey, who now lives in England, recently raised money to buy a lifeboat for a station on

*Avis Dolphin as an
elderly woman*

*Alice Lines and Audrey Pearl holding
hands as elderly women*

the southern Irish coast in memory of her late mother and of her
two lost sisters.

George, Elsie, and Frank Hook remembered the attack on
the *Lusitania* for the rest of their lives. They never forgot how for-
tunate they had been to survive. So many family groups had lost
one member or more. The newspapers were full of pictures of the
tragic Crompton family from Philadelphia. The entire family—
both parents and six children—had died. The Williams family,
befriended by the Hooks, had only two survivors, Edith and her
seven-year-old brother, Edward. For the rest of her life Edith was
haunted by the memory of her little sister Florence's hand slipping
through hers as the waves pulled them apart.

Elizabeth Duckworth also knew how lucky she had been. Though still weak from her ordeal, she summoned up the grit to report for war work at an ammunition factory in England. She later returned to America and, after a worrisome five-hour wait on Ellis Island, was readmitted. She died in 1955 at age ninety-two, one of the true heroines of the sinking of the *Lusitania*.

Danish women and children on the hull of the U-20

Gerda Nielson and Jack Welsh, who had fallen in love on the ship and had saved each other's lives, married within a week of the sinking and less than two weeks after they first met. What happened later to Gerda and Jack is unknown.

Walther Schwieger, a hero to the German U-boat service, brought the *U-20* safely home to Germany in May 1915 after his mission. But in 1916 the *U-20* ran aground on the treacherous sandbanks off the coast of Jutland in Denmark. Schwieger was forced to abandon her after trying to blow her up. He did not want the U-boat, which had so famously sunk the *Lusitania*, to fall into the enemy's hands. Today, the *U-20*'s conning tower, where Schwieger was standing when he gave the order to fire on the *Lusitania*, is on view at the Strandingsmuseum at Thorsminde in Jutland. So is the *U-20*'s deck gun. Schwieger did not survive much longer himself. In 1917 his new U-boat, the *U-88*, was lost at sea with all hands, probably after hitting a British mine.

Parts of the *Lusitania* have also been salvaged. One of her giant bronze propellers sits like a great dinosaur bone outside the

Propeller of the
Lusitania *at*
Liverpool

Merseyside Maritime Museum in Liverpool. Deck chairs and salt-stained life jackets, menus, and crockery have also been rescued and put on display. The wreck itself, lying on its starboard side and gradually collapsing under the pressure of water, is protected by the Irish government.

Queenstown, now renamed Cobh (pronounced *Cōve*), looks little changed from the town that welcomed bedraggled, dripping Avis Dolphin, Professor Holbourn, Audrey and Stuart Pearl, Alice Lines, the Hook family, and so many others on the night of May 7, 1915. The same hotels are still there. So are Cunard's offices, just a stone's throw from the old White Star Line's offices, where the last passengers waited to board the *Titanic* for her ill-fated maiden voyage in 1912. The townspeople still remember the *Lusitania*. They hold services of commemoration, and the victims' graves are carefully tended. A few yards from Cunard's old offices is a beautiful memorial. An angel with a tranquil face stands with hands outstretched. The motto beneath reads, "Peace in God's name."

Memorial to the dead of the Lusitania

EPILOGUE

The final toll of the sinking of the *Lusitania* was 1,198 dead (or 1,201 if the three anonymous stowaways are included). Of the 1,257 passengers 785, including 128 Americans, were killed. Of the 702 crewmembers, 413 died.

Just like the attacks of September 11, 2001, on the World Trade Center, the sinking shocked the world. The sinking also had a big effect on what happened during the rest of World War I. People in the United States were horrified that the Germans had sunk a ship carrying women and children without warning and without first giving them a chance to get into the lifeboats, as international law said they must. They thought it was even worse that many of the dead were from the United States, a country with which Germany was not then at war. One American newspaper headline read, GERMANY SURELY MUST HAVE GONE MAD. Another paper said that "a pirate would apologize" for such an outrage, and a third that, unlike the German Navy, even a rattlesnake used its rattle to give a warning before attacking.

President Woodrow Wilson had "tears in his eyes" when he first heard the news, asking, "How could any nation calling itself civilized [do] so horrible a thing?" He and his cabinet protested very strongly to the German government. Germany at first defended her actions. She claimed that she had been entitled to attack the *Lusitania,* and that, by placing the advertisement in the newspaper, she had given a warning. However, dismayed at the angry reaction

Diagram of the number of deaths from the sinking

from so many countries around the world, Germany promised the American government that she would not sink any more passenger ships without warning. It was a promise she did not keep. German U-boats attacked several more passenger ships over the next eighteen months, and more Americans were killed.

"Lest We Forget"
British poster

In April 1917 the United States declared war on Germany. American soldiers marched into battle shouting, *"Lusitania!"* Recruitment posters were put up all over the country with the headline REMEMBER THE LUSITANIA! and showing passengers struggling in cold water beneath the single word ENLIST. Very many young Americans did so. One historian thought that although the *Lusitania* failed to bring her nearly 200 American passengers to Britain, her sinking brought 2 million American soldiers to Europe to defeat Germany.

"Enlist" poster

APPENDIX

FACTS ABOUT THE *LUSITANIA*

BUILDER: John Brown and Company, Clydebank, Scotland

LAUNCHED: June 7, 1906

MAIDEN VOYAGE: September 1907

LENGTH BETWEEN PERPENDICULARS: 760 feet

LENGTH OVERALL: 785 feet

BEAM (WIDTH): 88 feet

DRAFT: 34 feet

DEPTH: 60 feet

GROSS TONNAGE: 30,395 tons

NET TONNAGE: 12,611 tons

RIG: fore and aft

BOILERS: 25 cylindrical Scotch (23 doubled-ended, 2 single-ended) in 4 boiler rooms

FURNACES: 192 with total heating surface of 158,350 square feet

STEAM PRESSURE: 195 pounds per square inch

AVERAGE COAL CONSUMPTION: just under 1,000 tons a day

MACHINERY: 4 propeller shafts driven by Parsons steam turbines with a total power output of 68,000 horsepower (the propellers were 3-bladed until 1909, thereafter 4-bladed).

In writing this book, the author drew on her own longer account for adults, *Lusitania: An Epic Tragedy,* also published by Walker & Company. The experiences of the three children Avis Dolphin, Frank Hook, Audrey Pearl, and of their friends and family aboard the *Lusitania,* and all quotes attributed to them, are drawn from original sources:

⚙ The story of Avis Dolphin and Professor Holbourn comes from Avis Dolphin's interviews with the British Broadcasting Corporation (BBC) and her correspondence with Adolph and Mary Hoehling when they were researching their book in the 1950s (see below). This correspondence, together with letters from Professor Holbourn's wife, Marion, about her and her husband's experiences, is now held by the Mariners' Museum, Newport News. Professor Holbourn also described the sinking in his book *The Isle of Foula*, published in 1938 by Johnson and Greig in Lerwick, Scotland.

⚙ The story of the Hook family comes from interviews published in the newspapers of the time and from the Cunard company archives in Liverpool University, England.

⚙ The saving of baby Audrey Pearl by her nurse Alice Lines, and the fate of the rest of the Pearl family, is described in evidence given by Audrey's father and mother, Major Warren and Mrs. Amy Pearl, after the sinking (now in the U.S. National Archives, Maryland), in an interview given by Audrey Pearl (now Audrey Lawson-Johnson) and Alice Lines to *National Geographic*

(April 1994; see below), and in recent conversations between the author and Mrs. Lawson-Johnson.

The experiences of other passengers and crew are from interviews given to the press and the authorities after the sinking and, in some cases, from their subsequently published memoirs. In particular the comments of Cunard's New York agent Charles Sumner about the submarine threat to the ship and the description of events the day the *Lusitania* sailed are from newspaper reports of the time; quotes from bellboy Ben Holton and from cook George Wynne come from their interview with the BBC; quotes from bride Lucy Taylor are from her interview with the Canadian Broadcasting Corporation; widow Elizabeth Duckworth's story is told in papers in the Hoehling archive, Mariners' Museum, Newport News; Boston bookseller Charles Lauriat told his story in his book *The* Lusitania's *Last Voyage,* published by Houghton Mifflin, Boston, 1915; seaman Leslie Morton's comments come from his evidence in inquiries after the sinking and from his book *The Long Wake*, published by Routledge, London, 1968; Captain Turner's comments are from evidence he gave to various inquests and inquiries.

The comments of U.S. consul Wesley Frost about the sinking, rescue, and aftermath are from his account *German Submarine Warfare,* published by D. Appleton, London, 1938, and from his dispatches in the U.S. National Archives, Maryland.

The experiences of those in the rescue fleet are also all from original sources. In particular, the sad comments of the men of the Courtmacsherry lifeboat are from their subsequent report, now in the Cobh Museum, Ireland.

The descriptions of life aboard a U-boat come from eyewitness accounts of U-boatmen, in particular those published in K. Neureuther and C. Bergen's book *U-Boat Stories,* published in translation by Constable, London, 1931.

Details of the voyage of the *U-20* are from the war diary of her captain Walther Schwieger, German military archive, Freiburg, Germany. His personal comments on the sinking are from a personal conversation with a friend recorded in L. Thomas's book *Raiders of the Deep*, published by William Heinemann, London, 1929.

The remarks of President Wilson on learning of the sinking were recorded by his secretary Joe Tumulty in his book *Woodrow Wilson As I Know Him,* Doubleday, New York, 1921.

SUGGESTED FURTHER READING

R. D. Ballard. *Exploring the Lusitania*. New York: Warner/ Madison Press, 1995. An account of Bob Ballard's recent exploration of the wreck of the *Lusitania,* with excellent pictures of the wreck.

A. A. Hoehling and M. Hoehling. *The Last Voyage of the Lusitania*. Lanham, Md.: Madison Books, 1996. An account of the liner's last voyage, based on interviews with survivors in the 1950s.

National Geographic, April 1994. A highly illustrated account of the sinking and the search for the wreck.

ART CREDITS

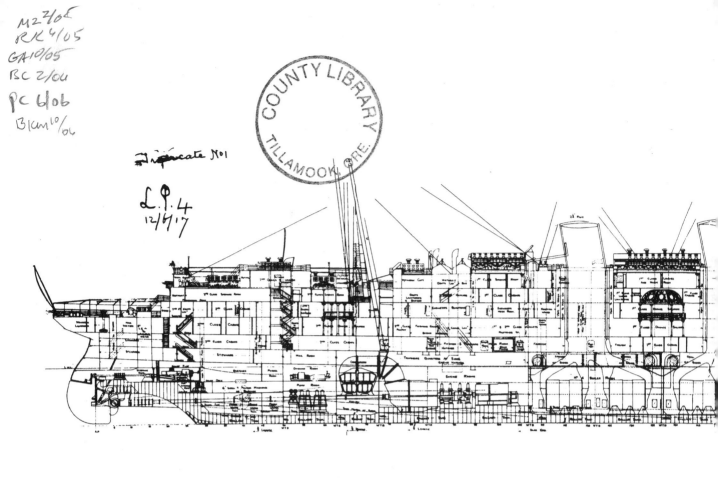

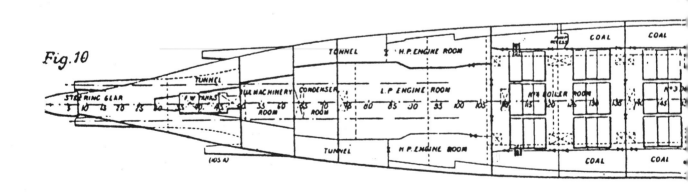

Fig.10